COLORS OF SERENITY

A Comprehensive Acrylic Art Therapy Guide for Beginners

Vicki Ruby

Table of Contents

CHAPTER ONE

INTRODUCTION

Workmanship treatment is an arrangement of inventive clarification that hopes to help individuals recuperate and feel basically gotten to a higher level. Craftsmanship treatment assists individuals with inspecting their opinions, develop care, conform to pressure, help assurance, and work on instinctive limits. This can give individual data and empower new procedures for overseeing pressure. Assuming you are new to the chance of Craftsmanship Treatment under is an adolescent's guide that I want to acknowledge that you will consider huge.

WHO CAN PROFIT FROM WORKMANSHIP TREATMENT

Anybody could maybe profit from workmanship treatment, no matter what the way that it will not really be for everybody and there are different kinds of treatment to look at to suit a single's necessities. Workmanship treatment can be significant solid areas for an of treatment that is reasonable for all ages from almost no kids to grown-ups to the old. It very well may be especially important for people who have expected to face testing issues in their lives, for example, precious, social, or near and dear medical problems, learning or genuine weakens, unsafe issues, neurological circumstances, and authentic ailments or to assist with the injury of wretchedness. Workmanship treatment doesn't need creative breaking point, yet it will overall be a fundamentally fixing process. In the event that somebody feels that workmanship treatment could help them, I would propose looking for the heading of an expert educated authority.

MY SPECIALTY TREATMENT OUTING

For quite a while I have felt that making magnum opus can be productive to an individual's psychological thriving. Right when I was at school, I worked with youngsters at a nearby school, looking at feelings and empowering them to make craftsmanship that could hear their thoughts. when I went through a time of serious individual injury that my resources pulled in me to making creative work as a bit by bit process for getting by and changed into a kind of treatment that has occurred through to now. During work, I encountered a tremendous extent of blood disaster. Straightforwardly following being hustled to office for a crisis cesarean, different immensely awful hours in a little while. For certain, even in those early days, I would see clear pictures that I expected to draw, however around then, I didn't have the guts to put pen to paper. This was my most fundamental experience of genuine horrendous misery and I grasped how veritable harshness is, how your heart really harms and I felt a strain in my stomach that caused me to feel like I could at emphatically no point anytime have the decision to stand upright later on. As the months passed, I began to make notes and draws of my viewpoints and sentiments. It was an uncommonly normal association and became supportive for me. I similarly began rehearsing yoga much more routinely and I appear to take advantage of a relative bit of harsh criticism while I'm rehearsing yoga or making craftsmanship, they eventually remain solidly related for myself and brief me to feel nearer to my little girl who passed on. On the contrary side of this, I at this point have two unmistakable young women who worth making gem, in the way that different kid do, and we dependably do enunciations and qualities together. It's something that I have progressed a cognizant undertaking to create and I unequivocally recognize it goes along with us as a family. From this extremely ordinary spot, making gem is at this point a focal piece of my life and the presence of my family and has driven me to explore Craftsmanship Treatment in more detail.

CHAPTER TWO

CRAFTSMANSHIP TREATMENT AT HOME

As alluded to over, the course of a coordinated master ought to be looked for while investigating workmanship treatment to guarantee that the strategies are utilized to treat express circumstances. Notwithstanding, there are various ways workmanship can be utilized at home to ease pressure and foster a decent impression of thriving and care. Such procedures could include:

• Crucial Circles - You basically need a pen or pencil and something to draw on. Start by loosened up drawing a little circle on the page, endeavoring to finish the circle.

Then, go over this cycle on different occasions, utilizing more noteworthy and more unpretentious circles, permitting them to join each other on the page or maybe in any case, investigating with winding shapes. Each time, taking it gradually.

• Compose Drawing - You basically need a piece of paper and a pen, pencil or pastel. These materials can be changed, as liked. This technique consolidates shutting your eyes and essentially forming over the paper. This cycle can be continued to utilize various combinations and once finished could be taken further by making a picture inside the jotting or hiding in the various shapes.

• Making montages from your own designs - Utilize any paints that are available to you, and any paper, cardboard or other material to make an image. Right when your image is finished, cut it or annihilate it into states of your decision, for example stripes or squares or just torn bits of any size. Then, at that point, utilize the pieces of the chief piece to look at and make a construction as another piece of craftsmanship.

• Body prints - Basically paints and paper are ordinary in this development no brushes are required. The object of this exercise is to utilize a piece of your body to make a craftsmanship piece. This could be your hand, fingers, finger nails, toes, feet any piece of the body can be utilized. Then, utilize the states of your body to make a genuinely remarkable convincing work of art.

• Bubble painting - For this development, you will require cleaning up fluid, paint, cups, straws and paper. Blend the paint and washing fluid in a cup and consequently blow climbs through a straw. Lay some paper over the air pockets to make a scratching and rehash on different occasions with various collections. Maybe also pour paint/rises on the paper and utilize the straw to blow or move the paint around and analyze various shapes. You could explore point of view tones to bestow your sentiments.

ADVANTAGES OF CRAFTSMANSHIP TREATMENT

Workmanship as-treatment assists process feelings, support with charactering, and divert from uneasiness. Workmanship treatment most frequently depicts the most notable way to deal with working with a coordinated craftsmanship prepared proficient. In a clinical setting, workmanship treatment can cause a diminishing in consequences of trauma, 1 depression, 1 and character disorders.2 Formal craftsmanship treatment creates precious consideration and rule, supports character, and constructs changing limits. Every so often formal craftsmanship treatment is called workmanship in-treatment, as seen from solo workmanship as-treatment. Certainly, even without an expert in the room, practicing your imaginative psyche has giant restorative benefits.3 Assessments of loosened up craftsmanship rehearses found that they worked with critical dealing with and refreshed self-worth, 4 as well as working with strain and exhaustion. We realize not every person can get to a specialist. While we can't ensure similar health advantages, we actually think workmanship on its own will compensate. You can utilize craftsmanship to comprehend and communicate your gloomy feelings or treat it as a serene excursion from your concerns. Give any of the accompanying workmanship as-treatment practices a shot!

WORKMANSHIP TREATMENT ACTIVITIES

In the event that you don't know what exercise will turn out best for you, pick one where you knew all about the medium, or pick the one you have an inquisitive outlook on. Each exercise ought to work for a fledgling. On the off chance that a clear page worries you, a blended media collection is a simple way for anybody to begin making. Cut makegraphs from magazines and stick them down with a paste pen to cause fantastical situations. You can likewise integrate explores different avenues regarding different media cut up works of art or drawings you weren't happy with and make a novel, new thing. On the off chance that you make an excessive number of collections, pop them into envelopes and mail them to distant companions.

CONCEPTUAL WATERCOLOR PAINTING

Theoretical watercolor painting is a tactile enjoyment of movement and variety. Watercolors love to stream and combine as one, which makes them ideal for wonderful, amazing dynamic work of art. We suggest Kuretake Gansai Tambi watercolors, which contain profoundly pigmented paints and arrive in a scope of sizes and price tags. Match them with enormous paper to empower large, free movements, delicate Illustrious and Langnickel Harmony Brushes, and a blending range. Plunging a brush into water and watching twirls of paint float away is practically reflective. While working with watercolor, calculate evaporating time and clean time.

Work out: Take a page from the theoretical expressionists and activity canvases and investigate development without worry for the completed item. Take a stab at blotching, flicking, or sprinkling. What imprints do various developments make?

Suggestions: Kuretake Gansai Tambi Watercolor Ranges, Regal and Langnickel Harmony Brushes, Yasutomo Porcelain

Range, Worldwide Workmanship Liquid 100 Watercolor Paper

MARKER DRAWING

A most loved toy may be a decent model for this continued drawing exercise. Tom bow Double Brush Pens will open your creative mind. Their twofold finished development gives you a lot of choices toward one side, their long, swishy brush tips can make splendid fields of variety or natural lines and on the other, their stiffer projectile tips give you admittance to extraordinary detail. For a drawing experience that joins parts of both, attempt Pentel Sign Pens. Their springy tips are enjoyable to outline with at a limited scale.

We like markers for their clear tone with no wreck and for the authoritativeness of their lines. When you put a discount, it stays down! Working without an eraser shows you the significant ability of integrating lines that go awkward as opposed to worrying about flawlessness. Over the long run, your certainty will thrive.

Work out: Get a treasured item and fill a page by drawing it over and over. With improved on colors, regardless of whether each sketch is free and chaotic, the entire page will in any case look bound together.

Suggestions: Tombow Double Brush Pens, Pentel Sign Pens, Worldwide

SHADED PENCIL DRAWING

Figuring out how to consolidate various surfaces makes a calming condition of concentration. Hued pencils give fulfilling material criticism as their tips delicately rub against paper. We propose putting resources into Prismacolors, our inside and out most loved shaded pencil. They're exceptionally obscure and lavishly pigmented, and that implies no dissatisfaction while setting down lines or filling in a space with variety. Prismacolors are fabulous on conditioned and shaded paper, and will look perfect on any paper or cardboard with gentle tooth. Make certain to have a sharpener close by!

Work out: Integrate however many surfaces as could be expected under the circumstances. Take a stab at crosshatching, texturing, and scumbling to begin. Cross-over surfaces and varieties to make amazing mixes.

Suggestions: Prismacolor Head Variety Pencils, Stillman and Birn Nova Sketchbook, Uni Variety Pencil Sharpener, Sakura Sumo Hold Retractable Eraser

WORKMANSHIP JOURNALING

Finding opportunity to consider your day can turn into a consoling custom.

On the off chance that workmanship quiets you down, think about making it a customary piece of your life. Keeping a diary on your bedside table or hauling it around with you will mean you're constantly ready. Its speck lattice continues composing perfect however doesn't forestall doodling or other representation, and its smooth, meager pages don't show any bleed through or padding while composing with ink.

Sakura Pigma Micron Pens are documented quality, so you can think back on your diaries long into the future, and are accessible in a scope of varieties and exact tip sizes. Or on the other hand, to treat yourself, diary with a wellspring pen. The input of a metal nib against the page gives a charming, establishing material sensation. For a fabulous prologue to the universe of wellspring pens, get a Pilot Metropolitan. It very well might be scary to begin a diary however our manual for journaling contains a lot of tips and procedures to assist you with slipping into the training.

Work out: Depict an occasion in your day, drawing or cartooning the parts you thought often the most about. On the off chance that you develop the propensity and diary reliably, a workmanship diary will be a successful state of mind tracker as well as a vault of prized recollections.

GROWN-UP SHADING BOOKS

One more method for keeping away from the feeling of dread toward a clear page: begin with a shading book. While they give less chances to put yourself out there, they assist you gain experience with your specialty supplies, and filling in intricate lines can make a quieting "stream express." Pepin Shading Books allow you the opportunity to reconsider exemplary masterpieces, with enough detail that you can undoubtedly sink hours into one page.

CHAPTER THREE

THOUGHTFUL WORK OF ART FOR STRESS HELP AND RECUPERATING

Reflective composition is an approach to delivering pressure and negative energy through the craft of painting. It is a contemplation practice that can be utilized to recuperate your life. You needn't bother with to be a specialist or an expert painter to involve painting as a treatment. There are no set standards, truth be told! You are essentially going to assemble your feelings and delivery them on a material without passing judgment on your work and without stressing over the final product.

Any type of medium and way of painting can be utilized for reflective painting, for example, watercolor painting, acrylic pouring, and pencil drawing, and so on. Utilize anything that medium you might want to utilize. The entire motivation behind this reflection cycle isn't to zero in on the medium, the method, or even the outcome, yet rather center around loosening up the psyche, quieting the spirit, and relinquishing your pessimistic feelings.

Today, I will tell you the best way to do an astounding thoughtful artistic creation work out; Acrylic pouring to music.

REFLECTIVE ARTISTIC CREATION EXERCISE

In this activity, you will figure out how to paint by feeling; that is, you will permit your creative ability to be directed by music. So how would you do this? Indeed, you should depend on the thing you are feeling while at the same time paying attention to the picked music, and afterward permit those sentiments to direct you while picking your varieties and pouring your paints. Yet, before we delve into additional subtleties, we should discuss the materials that you should begin.

Materials You Will Need:

• Acrylic paints-These ought to be fit to-be-poured paints (paints + pouring medium).

Use Coupon Code loveacrylicpainting621 to get 20% OFF

On the off chance that you are new to acrylic pouring and don't have any idea how to blend your acrylic paints with pouring medium to get them to the right consistency, then, at that point

STEP BY STEP INSTRUCTIONS TO PAINT TO MUSIC

1. Choose a very place where you can paint undisturbed.

2. Have a bunch of fit to-be poured paints before you.

3. Choose a piece of music that you find unwinding or that gives you pleasure! Begin playing the music.

4. While paying attention to the music you picked, begin picking 3-5 varieties in light of what you feel. Allow that music to direct you into picking the varieties that you will use for your artwork.

5. Start pouring your tones onto your material in any irregular manner that you'd like. Pour them in lines, circles, or puddles; or put every one of your varieties in a cup and afterward pour. Allow your imaginative ability to be directed by the music you are paying attention to.

6. Tilt your material to make your paints stream and cover your material.

7. Now, while your paint is as yet wet, you can add some sparkle, rocks, jewel chips, or some other embellishments you'd like. This is discretionary however can make your artistic creations truly stick out! Add embellishments to your pour assuming you feel like it!

8. Let your composition dry on a level surface.

THE END

www.ingramcontent.com/pod-product-compliance
Lightning Source LLC
Chambersburg PA
CBHW060907260726
48661CB00008B/3515